# PICTUREPEDIA

## NOTE TO PARENTS

This book is part of PICTUREPEDIA, a completely
new kind of information series for children.
Its unique combination of pictures and words
encourages children to use their eyes to discover and
explore the world, while introducing them to a wealth
of basic knowledge. Clear, straightforward text
explains each picture thoroughly and provides
additional information about the topic.

'Looking it up' becomes an easy task with
PICTUREPEDIA, an ideal first reference for all types of
schoolwork. Because PICTUREPEDIA is also entertaining,
children will enjoy reading its words and looking
at its pictures over and over again. You can encourage and
stimulate further inquiry by helping your child
pose simple questions for the whole family to
'look up' and answer together.

# SPORT

# DK

A DORLING KINDERSLEY BOOK

**Consultant** Stan Greenberg

**Senior Editor** Sue Leonard
**Art Editor** Amanda Carroll

**Series Editor** Sarah Phillips
**Series Art Editor** Ruth Shane

**Picture Researcher** Miriam Sharland

**Production Manager** Ian Paton

**Editorial Director** Jonathan Reed
**Design Director** Ed Day

First published in Great Britain in 1994
by Dorling Kindersley Limited
9 Henrietta Street
London WC2E 8PS

Reprinted 1997 (twice)

Copyright © 1994 Dorling Kindersley Limited, London

Visit us on the World Wide Web at
http://www.dk.com

A CIP catalogue record for this
book is available from the British Library.

ISBN 0-7513-5116-4

Reproduced by Colourscan, Singapore
Printed and bound in Italy by Graphicom

# SPORT

## DORLING KINDERSLEY

LONDON • NEW YORK
STUTTGART

# CONTENTS

# THE WORLD OF SPORT

Every four years the world's greatest athletes compete in the Olympics. At every Olympic Games competitors run faster, jump higher and create more amazing records. The Olympic ideals of honesty, sportsmanship and pride flourish alongside these inspiring performances and spill over into the world of sport at every level.

**Source of Light**
The Olympic flame is carried by torch by a series of runners, from Olympia in Greece to the Games arena.

*Wreath*

*Kenyan runner William Tanui*

*Medal*

**The Ultimate Prize**
At the original Olympics in Ancient Greece winners received an olive wreath. Modern Olympic champions receive a gold medal.

*New Zealand showjumper Mark Todd*

**Old Events**
Some sports were once played at the Games but are now no longer included. For example, cricket was only played at the 1900 Games in Paris, France, when Britain beat France in the final.

## New Addition

New sports can be added to the Games. Windsurfing was only 20 years old when it became an Olympic event in 1984 – making it the youngest sport ever to be included.

## The Paralympic Games

Sport should be for everyone regardless of disabilities. The first full Paralympic Games were staged in Rome, Italy, in 1960. When possible, these games are held in the same country as the Olympics.

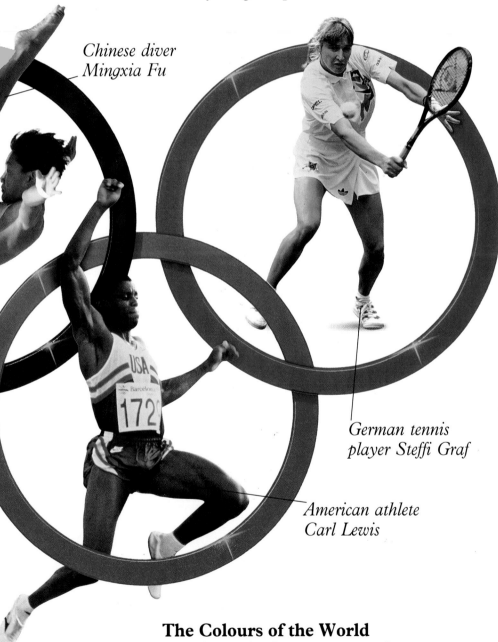

*Chinese diver Mingxia Fu*

*German tennis player Steffi Graf*

*American athlete Carl Lewis*

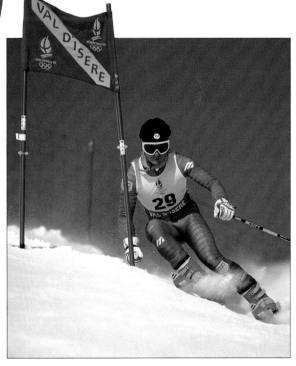

## The Winter Olympics

The first modern Olympics were held in Athens, Greece, in 1896. It was not until 1924 that the winter Olympics began in Chamonix, France. They are now held two years after the summer Games.

## The Colours of the World

The Olympic rings represent the five competing continents of the world. The flags of every Olympic nation contain at least one of the colours featured on the rings.

# RUNNING

As long as you are fit you can compete in running and chasing games. But world-class athletes have to train every day as they try to run faster than anyone has ever run before. Different running events require different physical abilities. Runners in the 100 metres produce amazing bursts of speed over short distances. Marathon runners have to keep a relatively constant speed during races that last for hours on end.

## Royal View

The 1908 Olympic Games were held in London, England. The marathon was run over 42,195 metres so that it could start beneath the royal children's nursery at Windsor Castle. This later became the standard distance.

## Record Run

On May 6, 1954, Roger Bannister was the first man to run a mile (1.609 km) in under four minutes.

*200, 3,000 and 5,000 metres start*

*Long-distance runners often break away from the rest of the field in the hope that the other runners will not be able to catch up.*

*The starter calls 'on your marks' and 'set'. Then he or she fires the starting pistol and the athletes burst into action.*

*110-metre hurdles start*

*100 metres and 100-metre hurdles start*

*For shorter distances athletes use starting blocks, which help them to push off.*

*Relay events are usually run over 4 x 100 metres or 4 x 400 metres. Three team members have to pass a baton to the next runner at the end of their leg of the race. The fourth runner crosses the finish line.*

## Making a Splash

Steeplechase runners jump four wooden barriers and a water jump on each of the race's seven full laps. Unlike hurdles, these barriers cannot be knocked over.

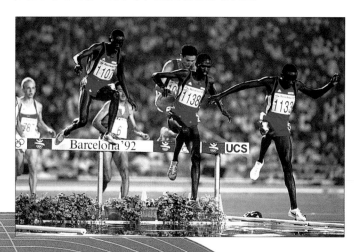

## On the Right Track

A standard athletics track is 400 metres around and all races are run anticlockwise. Modern tracks are made of synthetic materials and are not affected by the weather.

*Runners have spikes on the soles of their shoes that help them to grip the track.*

*1,500 metres start*

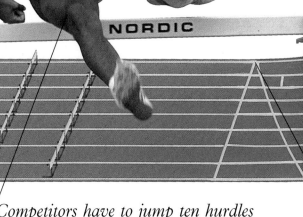

*Competitors have to jump ten hurdles for each race. In each event the hurdles are a different height. The hurdles in the 400 metres are the lowest.*

*Relays, 400-metre hurdles, 400, 800 and 10,000 metres start, and the finish for all races*

*100 metres runners are the fastest men and women on earth. Top sprinters reach speeds of over 40 kilometres an hour.*

# DECATHLON

The decathlon contest is made up of ten track and field events. Contestants have to be very fit and skilled in order to take part in so many different running, jumping and throwing competitions. Many of the events date back to the original Games held at Olympia in Greece some 3,000 years ago. Modern decathletes battle against each other in order to find out who is the best all-round sportsman in the world.

**Testing Time**
The ten decathlon events are held over two days.

100 metres   Long jump   Shot put   High jump   400 metres

110-metre hurdles   Discus   Pole vault   Javelin   1,500 metres

**Training for War**
Javelin and discus throwing were both part of the ancient Olympic Games. At that time sport was a way of training for battle. The javelin was a throwing weapon and the discus developed from a shield.

*A javelin weighs 800 grams and is between 260 and 270 centimetres long.*

*A discus weighs two kilograms.*

**Heavy Weight**
Male athletes use a shot weighing over seven kilograms – the same as this basket of potatoes. The shot, javelin and discus used by women are lighter than those used by the men.

*A shot weighs 7.26 kilograms.*

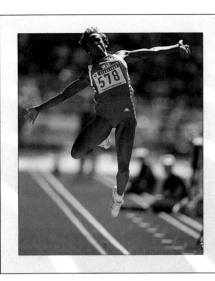

## Heptathlon
The women's version of the decathlon is called the heptathlon. The women compete in seven events over two days: 100-metre hurdles, high jump, shot put, 200 metres, long jump, javelin, and 800 metres.

## The Pole Vault
The pole is about five metres long and is made of fibreglass. Top pole vaulters have managed to clear heights of over six metres.

*Once he has pushed off from the ground the vaulter hangs from the pole to make it bend.*

*Vaulters often put tape around the pole to help them to get a good grip.*

*The vaulter starts running towards the crossbar with the pole held almost upright. As he runs he lowers the end of the pole towards the ground.*

*The vaulter plants the pole in the vaulting box – a sloping metal box set into the ground in front of the landing mat.*

*The crossbar is placed on supports on the uprights. It is winched up to the required height.*

*As the pole straightens it powers the vaulter upwards. He does a handstand and prepares to throw himself over the crossbar.*

*The landing mat is filled with foam.*

# GYMNASTICS

If you can do a cartwheel, a handstand or play leapfrog then you are a gymnast! To be a champion gymnast requires complete dedication and a mixture of grace and strength. Competitors have to be able to somersault and spin across the floor exercise mat, and leap on and off the apparatus with amazing confidence.

*Female gymnasts wear skin-tight, long-sleeved leotards made of stretchy material. They let them move around easily.*

*Gymnasts keep their hair tied back so that it does not get in the way.*

*Competitors put chalk on their hands to help them grip.*

### Rhythmic All-Around

Rhythmic gymnastics was first included in the Olympic Games in Los Angeles, USA, in 1984. Competitors do jumps, skips, hops and spirals to music, using ropes, hoops, balls, clubs and ribbons. The ribbon the gymnasts use is six metres long and is very hard to control.

*The beam is padded and covered in suede. It is five metres long, 1.2 metres high and only ten centimetres wide.*

### Women's Floor Exercise

Gymnasts perform the most incredible tumbles, handstands and cartwheels as they spring across the floor.

*This gymnast shows remarkable balance as she holds her body in a dramatic arched position.*

## Age Advantage
The younger you are the easier it is to do basic gymnastic positions, like the splits. Many top gymnasts are only in their early teens.

## Full Flight
Gymnasts swing round and round on the asymmetric bars, then let go to move from one bar to another.

## Hanging Around
Male gymnasts have to do a handstand while competing on the rings. To perform a move like this requires great strength.

## Swinging, Jumping and Balancing
As well as performing floor exercises, gymnasts compete on many different pieces of apparatus.

Women's Apparatus

Vault    Beam    Asymmetric bars

Men's Apparatus

Parallel bars    Vault    Horizontal bar    Pommel horse    Rings

# MARTIAL ARTS

All over the world sports have developed from people fighting each other. Most of these sports are now controlled so that the contestants hurt themselves as little as possible – boxers wear padded gloves and fencers have protective tips on the end of their swords. Some martial arts of the East, such as judo and karate, are only meant to be used as a method of self defence and self control.

### Sumo Wrestling

In Japan top sumo wrestlers are treated like superstars. In a fight the wrestlers use their enormous bulk to try to push each other right out of the combat circle. Hawaiian-born wrestler Konishiki, known as the Dump Truck, weighs 225 kilograms. It would take nine small girls to equal his weight. The wrestlers eat huge amounts of a high-protein stew called *chanko-nabe*.

*Each contestant attempts to get the other off balance in order to throw them to the floor.*

### Judo

The aim of judo, which means 'the soft way', is not to hurt your opponent but to show skill in carrying out the different judo throws.

*A judo mat has to be thick enough to absorb the weight of falling bodies. The first technique beginners are taught is how to fall without injuring themselves.*

### Belt Up!

The colour of the belt worn by judo competitors shows how good they are. The grades range from white to yellow, orange, green, blue and brown. Then comes the famous black belt. Masters of the sport can progress beyond the black belt to a white-and-red-striped belt, and then to a red belt and finally back to a white belt again!

## Fencing

There are three swords used in fencing: the foil, épée and sabre. All of them have protective tips but contestants still wear strong clothes and a face mask to stop them from coming to any harm.

*Only the tip of the foil can be used to score points.*

## Kite Fighting

One combat sport that is unlikely to hurt anybody is kite fighting. Flyers use their kites to move the special glass-coated line backwards and forwards over their opponent's line. This cuts the line and sends the enemy kite spiralling out of control.

*The judo costume of jacket, trousers and belt is called the* judogi.

*The jacket has to be very tough because of all the tugging that goes on during a bout.*

*Competitors go barefoot on the mat, but they have to cover their feet as soon as they leave it.*

## Boxing

Many of the world's top boxers have been Olympic medal winners. The most famous boxer of all time is Muhammad Ali. He won a gold medal in 1960 at the Olympics in Rome, Italy.

## Karate

Contestants in karate hit out with their hands, arms and feet to score points.

# ARCHERY

Hitting a target with an arrow, a dart, or a bullet requires a lot of skill. To fire an arrow from a bow you also need to be strong enough to pull back the bowstring, which is incredibly tight. Modern target archery bows do not look much like the traditional type of bow used by the legendary archer Robin Hood. They are made of advanced materials such as carbon fibre and have a sight and stabilizers.

*Stabilizer*

*Arrows have a sharp metal tip at the front, and a groove at the back that slots over the bowstring.*

*Stabilizer*

**Field Archery**

In field archery the archers have to move around a course shooting at different-sized targets from unknown distances. The instinctive bows used in barebow field archery do not have any sights or stabilizers so they look more like a traditional bow.

*Archers keep their arrows in a holster-style pouch, or quiver, which hangs from a belt around the waist.*

*Instinctive bow*

*The shorter the bow the faster the arrow flies, but longer bows are easier to control.*

## Target Archery

In target archery competitors shoot at one target from various distances.

*The sight is adjusted so that when the archer lines it up with the target the arrow should hit the place he or she is aiming at.*

### Shooting

Rifle-shooting competitors fire at unmoving targets. Rapid-fire pistol shooting targets are only turned towards the competitor for a few seconds. Free pistol shooters have two and a half hours to fire 60 shots at unmoving targets. Competitors at a clay pigeon shoot use shotguns to fire at airborne clay targets.

*Clay pigeon*

*Clay pigeon shooter*

Rapid-fire pistol target

Rifle target

Free pistol target

*Stabilizers are attached to the bow to help keep it steady while shooting.*

JAQUES

### On Target

Archery targets, known as butts, are made of straw ropes that are stitched together. Coloured paper or canvas targets are pinned to the butts. The nearer an arrow lands to the centre of the target, the higher the score.

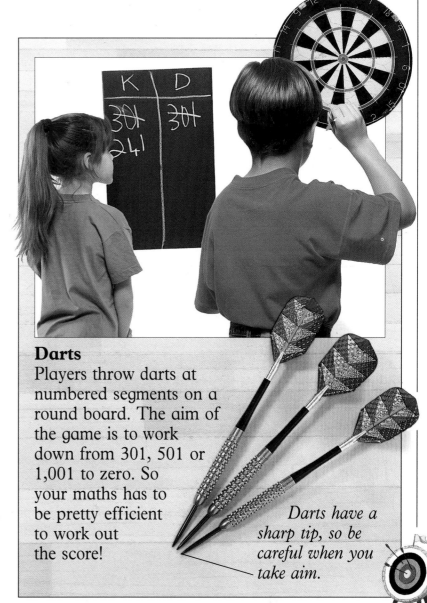

### Darts

Players throw darts at numbered segments on a round board. The aim of the game is to work down from 301, 501 or 1,001 to zero. So your maths has to be pretty efficient to work out the score!

*Darts have a sharp tip, so be careful when you take aim.*

# GOLF

There are a number of sports that involve throwing or rolling a ball – bowling, for example, and boules. There are other sports, such as golf or snooker, in which you use a stick to hit a ball. On a golf course, golfers use as few shots as possible to hit the ball from the tee, down the fairway, onto the green and into the hole. Golfers have major obstacles to deal with, including trees, rivers and big ditches, called bunkers, full of sand.

*To hit the ball hard, golfers raise the club up behind them. Then they take a big swing at the ball so that the club ends up behind their back.*

*Clubs with angled metal heads, known as irons, are used to make most of the shots.*

*Golfers wear shoes with spikes on the soles to help keep them steady when they swing at the ball.*

## Bowling Sports

In bowling, boules and bowls the aim of the game is to hit a target with a ball. In bowls, players roll the ball as near as possible to the target ball, or jack. Boules players throw the ball towards the jack. Bowlers roll the ball down an alley and try to knock over the pins standing at the end.

*Jack*

*Boules is played on a gravel surface.*

*Bowlers play on a wooden alley.*

*Bowls is normally played on grass.*

Pin

Jack

## Playing a Hole

*For his first shot, the player balances the ball on a holder called a tee peg.*

*Play starts with a drive, or tee shot, onto the fairway.*

*The fairway is a long stretch of shortish grass.*

18

*Players need to have a firm grip on the club and they wear a glove on one hand to help them.*

*One of the first techniques that golfers learn is how to hold the club correctly.*

## Golfing Hall of Fame
Here are some great golfing champions and their years at the top.

Bobby Jones
1920s

Ben Hogan
1940s and 1950s

Jack Nicklaus
1960s and 1970s

Seve Ballesteros
1970s and 1980s

## Winning Team
Fanny Sunneson is caddy for champion golfer Nick Faldo. Top caddies do more than carry the clubs – they know the world's major courses well and make suggestions on how to play each hole.

*Wood*

*Irons*

*Putter*

## Choosing a Club
There are three types of golf club: woods, irons and putters. Woods are for hitting the ball a long way. Irons are best for middle-distance shots up the fairway. Putters are designed for hitting the ball across the green and into the hole.

## Snooker
Snooker is played on a large cloth-covered table with six pockets. Players use a wooden cue to make a white ball hit the coloured balls. The aim is to knock these balls into the pockets.

*The golfer hits the ball down the fairway, trying to avoid the long grass, trees and bunkers. Unfortunately this ball lands in a bunker!*

*Finally the ball is pitched onto the green. The green is a smooth, grassy area where the golfer putts the ball into the hole.*

# TENNIS

Games such as tennis, squash and table tennis all involve hitting a ball between players. Tennis, in various forms, has been played for centuries, and its popularity continues to grow. It can be played indoors or outdoors by two people (singles), four people (doubles) and by men and women together (mixed doubles).

*1930s wooden tennis racket*

**Tennis Hall of Fame**
The championships held at the All England Tennis and Croquet Club, Wimbledon, London, are considered the greatest in the world. In their day these players made the event their own.

Elizabeth Ryan's record of 19 titles, set between 1914 and 1934, was only beaten by Billie Jean King in 1979.

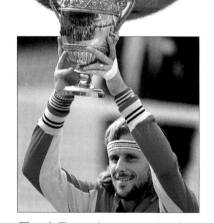

Fred Perry's record of three wins in a row between 1934 and 1936 was broken by Bjorn Borg in 1979.

*Modern rackets are designed by computer and are made of very strong, light materials such as graphite or fibreglass.*

*Players wear different types of shoes depending on the playing surface. Soles are pimpled for grass play.*

*Line judge*

*Wristbands and headbands help to soak up sweat during long, energetic games.*

*Tennis balls are made of hollow rubber covered with a fluffy layer of wool and man-made fibres.*

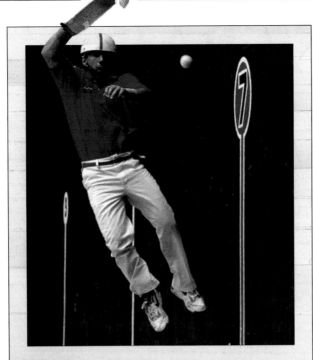

### Pelota
Pelota players use a wicker scoop to throw a ball against the walls of a court. The pelota ball can travel at over 290 kilometres an hour.

### Hit Records
Tennis player Steve Denton hit the fastest ever recorded serve of 222 kilometres an hour.

The fastest speed that a squash ball has travelled is 232 kilometres an hour.

Two table-tennis players rallied for a record-breaking 172 shots in 60 seconds.

Badminton is played with shuttlecocks. They can travel at nearly 200 kilometres an hour.

*This player is making a forehand shot. The three basic tennis strokes are serve, forehand and backhand.*

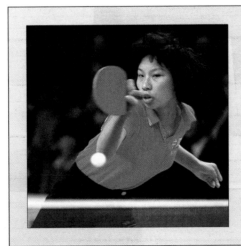

### Table Tennis
Table tennis was originally played with simple wooden bats. When the bats were given a rubber covering the players were able to spin the ball. The game then became more exciting and grew increasingly popular with players and spectators.

### The Court
Tennis court surfaces include grass, clay, concrete and asphalt.

Line judges

Umpire

Net-cord judge

Line judge

Singles sideline

Receiver

Baseline

Centre line

Service court

Net

Server

Ball person

Doubles sideline

# BASKETBALL

The team games of handball, volleyball and basketball are all action-packed and high scoring, and the players have to move incredibly quickly around the court. In basketball, two teams of five players try to throw the ball through the other team's basket. Players cannot run with the ball or kick it, but they are allowed to dribble, pass, throw or roll it, so they have to be extremely agile and very accurate – and it helps to be tall too!

*Players wear sleeveless shirts so that they can move their arms easily as they reach up above their heads to catch the ball.*

### Court Magicians

The Magicians of Basketball, as the world-famous Harlem Globetrotters are called, have been entertaining fans with their amazing trick shots for over 70 years.

### Fashionable Feet

Famous players like Michael Jordan help to design their own basketball boots, which are then produced for sale to the public.

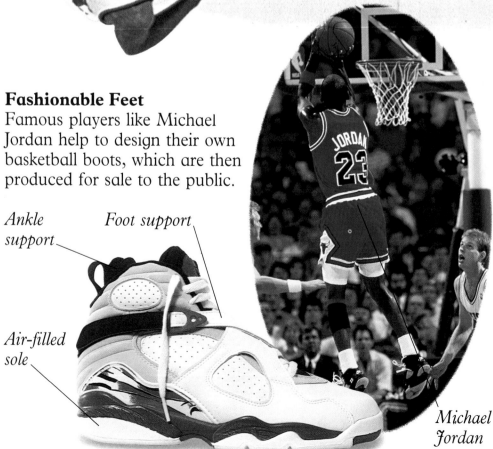

*Ankle support*

*Foot support*

*Air-filled sole*

*Michael Jordan*

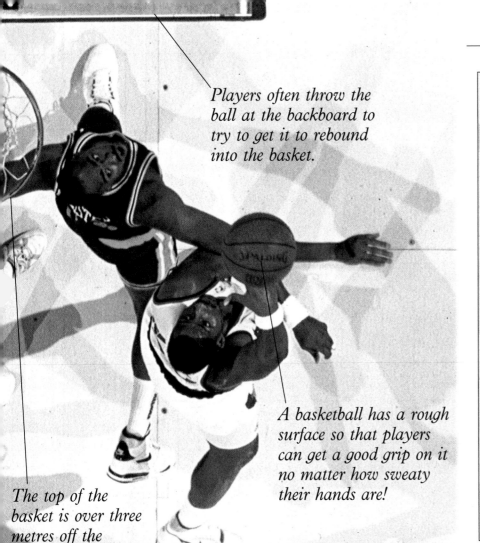

Players often throw the ball at the backboard to try to get it to rebound into the basket.

A basketball has a rough surface so that players can get a good grip on it no matter how sweaty their hands are!

The top of the basket is over three metres off the ground, but some players can jump high enough to drop, or dunk, the ball straight into the net.

Basketball has to be played on a hard surface so that the ball bounces well. A polished wooden surface is ideal.

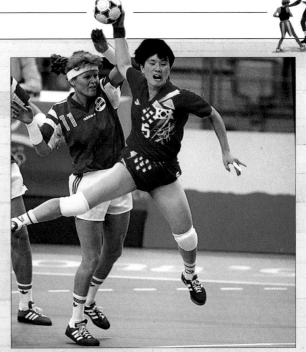

## Team Handball

Team handball is a fast and furious game that is a mix of basketball and soccer. The ball moves down the court in the same way as it does in basketball, but points are scored by throwing the ball into a goal.

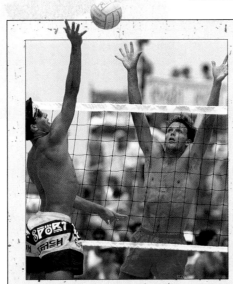

## Volleyball

Volleyball is played by two teams of six players on a hard court. Players use their hands to hit the ball over a high net. They try to keep the ball off the ground for as long as possible. Beach volleyball is played on sand and is regularly shown on television in America, where the sport is very popular.

## Dribble and Shoot

The player gets the ball but he cannot move unless he bounces it. This is known as dribbling.

He dribbles around an opponent.

He picks up the ball and jumps for the basket.

23

# SOCCER

Soccer is the most popular team game in the world. Eleven players on each side attempt to kick the ball into the other team's goal. The only member of the team who is allowed to touch the ball with his hands is the goalkeeper. Teams play for 45 minutes and have a 15-minute rest at half time. Then they swap ends and play for another, exhausting half lasting 45 minutes.

*The captain of a soccer team wears a coloured armband.*

## Sporting Supporters
You can buy child-sized versions of your country's national strip. But these strips change every few years, so keeping up to date with the latest style can be expensive.

*Players can be identified by the large number on the back of their shirt.*

## Massive Crowd
The world's largest soccer ground is the Estadio Maracana, in Rio de Janeiro, Brazil. The ground can hold up to 165,000 spectators.

*Balls used in top matches are made of leather panels, stitched together over an inflatable rubber inner ball.*

## Action From Goal to Goal
A soccer pitch is usually between 90 and 120 metres from end to end.

*The goalkeeper kicks the ball to one of his team.*

*This player runs with the ball before passing.*

*Goal line*

## The World Cup

Every four years the world's greatest soccer-playing countries compete for the World Cup. In 1970 the Brazilian team was allowed to keep the original cup after winning the competition for the third time. Teams now play for a new World Cup.

*A soccer player's strip, his shorts and shirt, has changed a lot over the years. Shorts have gone from baggy to tight and back to baggy again.*

*Players often wear shin guards underneath their socks to protect their legs during heavy tackles.*

*Soccer boots are very light to allow the player to run fast and to give him a good feel for the ball.*

## Soccer Hall of Fame

Here are eleven of the game's greatest players and the countries they played for.

Gordon Banks
England

Franco Baresi
Italy

Franz Beckenbauer
Germany

George Best
Northern Ireland

Bobby Charlton
England

Johan Cruyff
Holland

Eusebio
Spain

Diego Maradona
Argentina

Bobby Moore
England

Pelé
Brazil

Frank Rijkaard
Holland

*Corner flag*

*Attacker beats defender . . . then goalkeeper . . . and it's a goal!*

*Linesman*

*The referee makes sure the teams play by the rules.*

*The attacking players outwit the defence and move the ball up the pitch.*

*Goalkeeper*

# RUGBY AND AMERICAN FOOTBALL

The games of rugby and American football involve lots of physical contact. The players run with an oval ball and have to touch down over a line to score. They can also kick the ball between the tall goal posts to score points. The big difference is that rugby players are not allowed to pass the ball forwards, while American footballers can pass in any direction.

*American footballers wear a plastic helmet and face mask. Inside the helmet lots of small cushions fit snugly around the head.*

*American footballs have pointed ends to make them easier to throw.*

*Under his lightweight shirt this player has a plastic rib protector and huge shoulder and chest pads.*

**Dressing for Action**
American football players have to be well protected because they are allowed to make physical contact away from the ball.

*This player has a towel attached to his belt. He uses it to wipe his hands before each play.*

*Players wear tight, knee-length trousers that lace up at the front.*

*Hip, groin and thigh pads are worn underneath the trousers.*

**American Football Field**
American footballers play mainly on artificial turf, which is laid on top of a solid concrete base.

*American football boots are lightweight to help the players to run and turn quickly.*

*Starting line-up*

All sorts of pulling and tugging goes on in the rugby scrum so players often wrap tape around their head to protect their ears.

Players wear a basic kit of cotton shirt and shorts.

Rugby players protect their teeth with a special plastic gum shield.

Rugby balls have rounded ends.

## Rugby Pitch
Rugby players usually play on grass pitches. They often come off the field looking as though they have just taken a mud bath.

*Starting line-up*

## Australian Rules
Australian rules football is played by two teams of 18, on an oval pitch with four upright posts at each end. Players can kick, punch and run with the ball, but it has to touch the pitch, usually by bouncing, every ten metres.

*Rugby boots are made of tough leather and have studs on the soles to cope with slippery mud.*

*The quarterback waits to receive the ball.*

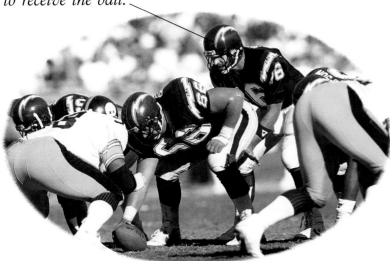

## The American Snap
In the snap players line up opposite each other. The team with the ball passes it to their quarterback who decides who to throw it to next.

## The Rugby Scrum
During a scrum the ball is put into a huddle of players from both teams. The teams push each other backwards. The players in the scrum use their feet to push the ball out to their scrum half.

*The scrum half waits for a chance to grab the ball.*

# BASEBALL

Baseball, softball, rounders and cricket have all developed from a basic bat-and-ball game that has been played since ancient times. All of these games involve hitting a ball with a bat and running between or around bases. The fielders have to return the ball in order to stop the runner's progress.

*Batter's helmet*          *Fielder's hat*

*The umpire-in-chief kneels right behind the catcher and decides if the balls have been pitched correctly.*

*Because the umpire is so close to the play he has to wear a protective mask.*

*The catcher wears a face guard, a chest protector and knee and shin guards.*

*The catcher's padded mitt helps him to catch the speeding ball if the batter misses it.*

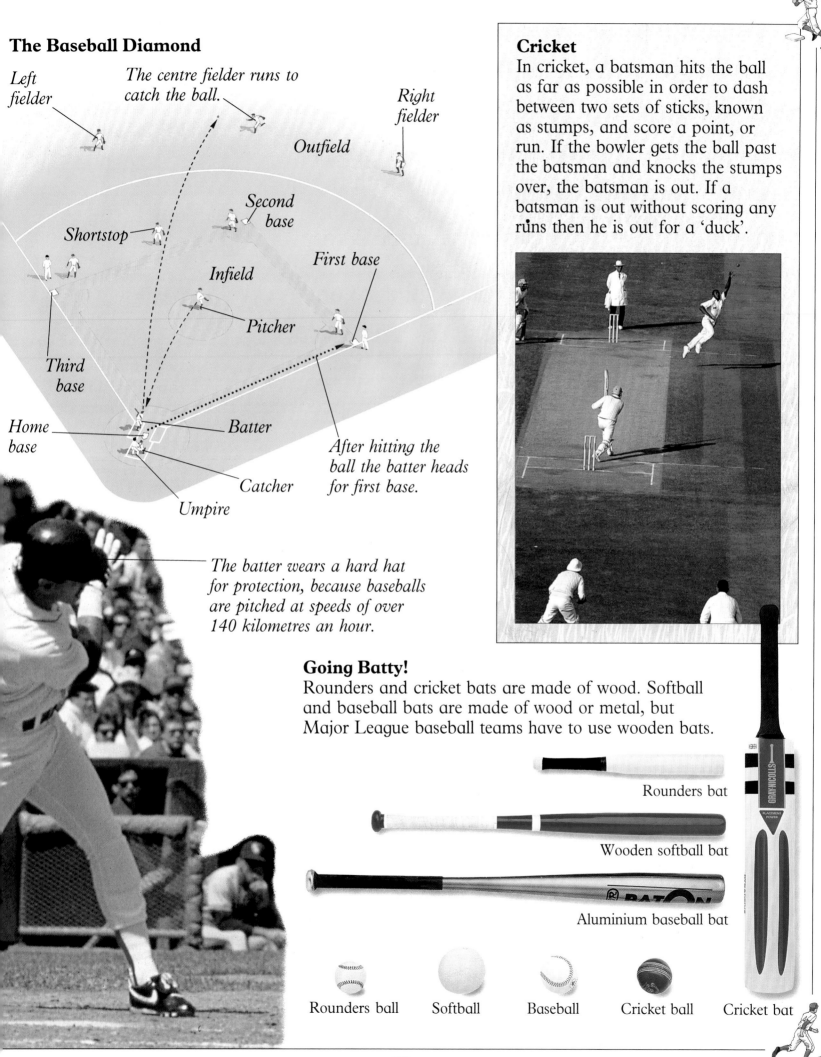

# The Baseball Diamond

Left fielder

*The centre fielder runs to catch the ball.*

Right fielder

Outfield

Second base

Shortstop

First base

Infield

Pitcher

Third base

Home base

Batter

*After hitting the ball the batter heads for first base.*

Catcher

Umpire

*The batter wears a hard hat for protection, because baseballs are pitched at speeds of over 140 kilometres an hour.*

## Cricket

In cricket, a batsman hits the ball as far as possible in order to dash between two sets of sticks, known as stumps, and score a point, or run. If the bowler gets the ball past the batsman and knocks the stumps over, the batsman is out. If a batsman is out without scoring any runs then he is out for a 'duck'.

## Going Batty!

Rounders and cricket bats are made of wood. Softball and baseball bats are made of wood or metal, but Major League baseball teams have to use wooden bats.

Rounders bat

Wooden softball bat

Aluminium baseball bat

Rounders ball    Softball    Baseball    Cricket ball    Cricket bat

# ICE HOCKEY

Ice hockey, like soccer, involves scoring goals by shooting an object into an opponent's net. But ice hockey players don't play with a ball, they use a rubber disc called a puck, and they hit it with a stick. The game is fast and furious and very physical, as the players speed across the ice and crash against each other. Roller hockey and field hockey are exciting too, and players show great skill as they control the ball while moving at high speed.

### Dangerous Position
The goalkeeper needs all the protection he can get when faced with a dangerous flying puck. He wears a chest protector under his shirt, a face mask and leg guards.

### Crushed Ice
An ice hockey game is split into three periods of 20 minutes. The ice takes a real bashing during a game. To make the surface smooth again a resurfacing machine trundles around the rink between periods.

### Crashing Around
The rink is surrounded by boards over a metre high. Spectators sitting just behind the boards are only centimetres from the action as the players crash into each other and the side boards.

*There are six members of each team.*

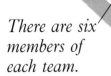

*The goal is not very big – just over a metre high and just under two metres wide.*

## Field Hockey

There are eleven players in a field hockey team. The game is usually played on grass. The head of a field hockey stick is tiny compared to that of an ice hockey stick.

## Roller Hockey

Roller hockey is played by teams of five. The players wear in-line skates or roller skates with a wheel on each corner.

*In-line skates have four wheels in a row and, as with ice hockey boots, you need a good sense of balance to use them.*

*Players wear all sorts of protective gear under their clothing, as well as padded gloves and hard hats.*

## Sinful Behaviour

When players disobey the rules the referee sends them off the ice and to the penalty bench, or 'sin bin', for up to ten minutes.

*The blades on ice hockey skates are shorter than on figure skates. This makes them safer and more manoeuvrable.*

*Ice hockey sticks are 135 centimetres long. Players are not supposed to swing their sticks above shoulder height – if they do they get sent to the sin bin.*

# FIGURE SKATING

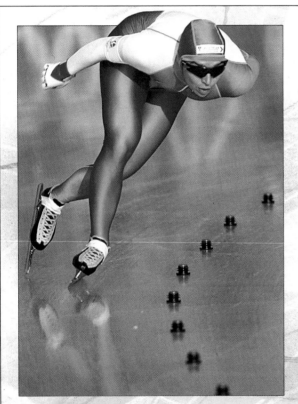

World-class figure skaters have to carry out extremely complicated, and dangerous, moves as part of their routines. Perhaps their greatest skill is that they make it look so easy. These skaters need a good sense of balance and plenty of confidence. They add speed, grace, strength and dancing ability to these qualities in order to create the most breathtaking routines. Speed skaters also show amazing control on the ice as they power around frozen tracks at up to 50 kilometres an hour.

*Figure skaters perform all sorts of twisting moves on the ice, often while skating very fast.*

*Skaters have to train constantly to achieve the level of fitness needed to make such physically demanding moves look effortless.*

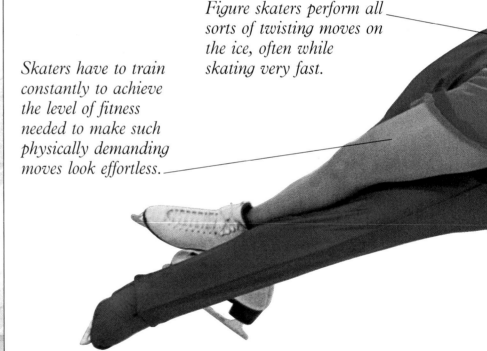

**Speed Skating**
Speed skaters race around the track in pairs, but they are actually racing against the clock rather than each other. They take swinging steps, throwing their arms from side to side to increase their speed. Their skintight suits and hats help them to slice through the air.

*Boots give plenty of ankle support.*

*The skates lace up from toe to ankle for a perfect fit.*

**Cutting Edge**
The blades on figure skates are grooved in the middle. This means that whichever way the skater is leaning, he or she is still balanced on a sharp cutting edge.

## Making Moves

There are three different types of figure skating competitions – single skating, pair skating and ice dancing. In all three, skaters perform routines containing certain set moves as well as routines containing steps they have chosen themselves.

Single skating

Pair skating

Ice dancing

*Some ice dance costumes are striking as they are designed to complement the music that the dancers skate to.*

## Up in the Air

This skater is doing a double Salchow jump. The skater jumps off the ice and does a double twist in the air before landing. This jump is named after Ulrich Salchow, who won the first men's Olympic figure skating gold medal in 1908.

*You can see how complicated these twists and turns are by looking at the marks the blades cut into the surface of the ice.*

## Perfect Partnership

In figure skating, the judges award marks out of six, depending on how good they think a performance is. In 1984, ice dancers Jayne Torvill and Christopher Dean made skating history when they became the first skaters ever to be awarded a row of nine perfect sixes at the Olympic Games.

6.06.06.06.06.06.06.06.06.0

# SKIING

The main things that skiing, ski jumping and bobsleigh have in common are snow, ice, speed and danger. Downhill skiers reach speeds of over 100 kilometres an hour as they fly down a mountain. Slalom skiers do not travel quite so fast, but they have to twist and turn around marker poles with incredible agility.

*Downhill racers wear protective helmets, because skiing is extremely dangerous at high speeds.*

*Ski poles help skiers to turn and keep their balance. Downhill skiers use poles that curve around the body.*

*Ski boots are made of strong plastic and give the foot and ankle plenty of support.*

## Snowboarding

A snowboard is a lot wider than a ski. Boarders do not use ski poles. Straps on the board do up over the top of their boots and they stand sideways, like a surfer. They wear wild clothes and do the most amazing jumps.

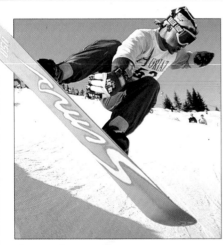

## Skiing Events

In skiing there are seven different types of competitive events.

*Skiers weave through a series of poles.*

*A combination of downhill and slalom skiing*

Downhill    Slalom    Giant slalom    Ski jumping

## Ski Jumping

A ski jump can be a terrifying 60 metres high. Judges in a tower give points for each skier's performance, taking into account the style and length of the jump.

*Racers wear skintight suits that do not catch the wind as they rush down the mountain.*

*The undersides of the skis are coated in wax to help them to slide over the snow.*

## Bobsleigh and Luge

A luge has no steering or brakes. A bobsleigh has a fibreglass shell, a steerable front runner and a brake that digs into the ice. Both speed down a treacherous icy track with high, curved sides.

*Luge*

*Two-man bobsleigh*

Suisse 1

## Skis and Boots

Cross-country equipment is much lighter than that used for downhill skiing.

*Downhill skis*

*Cross-country skis*

*The toe of a cross-country shoe is attached to a single binding on the ski.*

*Cross-country is done across uneven, snow-covered countryside.*

*Freestylers specialize in either ballet, jumping or racing down bumpy slopes called mogul fields.*

*Competitors ski cross-country and fire at targets along the way.*

*Clamps called bindings hold the boot onto the ski. The bindings release the ski during a fall.*

*Downhill boots*

*Cross-country shoes*

Cross-country

Freestyle skiing

Biathlon

# THREE-DAY EVENT

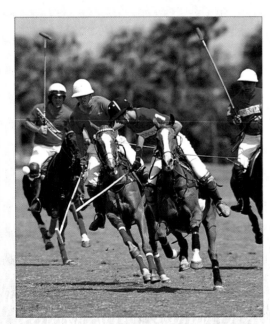

Competing in the three-day event is the ultimate test of a person's horsemanship. The first day's riding takes place in the hushed dressage arena. The second day's challenge is carried out on the long and tiring endurance course. Then, on the third day, horse and rider have to show themselves to be strong enough to clear the jumps on the tricky, winding showjumping course.

Dressage hat

Endurance hat

Showjumping hat

*Jumps can be up to 1.2 metres tall, which is probably as tall as you!*

*White breeches*

*Riders get penalty points if their horse knocks down part of an obstacle or refuses to jump.*

**Polo**
Polo is known as hockey on horseback. Two teams of four players thunder up and down the polo field. They attempt to use their long-handled mallets to hit the small polo ball between the goal posts. The owner of a polo team has to be very rich, as polo ponies are extremely expensive.

*Fancy gate*     *Hog's back*

*Water jump*

*Stone wall*

## Clearing the Jumps

The showjumping course is made up of between ten and twelve different jumps.

*The rider leans right forward in the saddle to help the horse to balance as it powers its way over the jump.*

*The reins are attached to the bit. When the rider pulls on the left or right rein, the horse turns in that direction.*

*Red hunting jacket*

*The leather bridle holds a metal bit in the horse's mouth.*

*The same horse takes part in each stage of the three-day event.*

## Dressage

In the dressage competition, riders aim to show that their horses follow their commands absolutely. At first it may appear dull, but if you look closely you can see how accurately the horse stops, starts and changes speed and direction.

## Endurance

The speed and endurance course involves riding across roads, paths and fields. Competitors ride over jumps, up and down steep slopes and over, or sometimes through, water. The course is 25 kilometres long and is fast-moving, muddy and dangerous.

# CYCLING

**Track Racing**
Track racers compete on an oval track with banked sides, called a velodrome. The arrival of the futuristic Lotus Superbike in Barcelona, Spain, for the 1992 Olympics put the sport in the headlines all over the world.

There is more to riding a bike than going from place to place. Mountain-bike racers tackle impossibly steep hills and ride through mud and water. Road racers cover enormous distances and ride for days on end. Track racers hurtle around an arena at speeds of up to 80 kilometres an hour, without any brakes or gears.

**Triathlon**
Triathletes swim, cycle and run, all in one event. In the Iron Man, the longest of the triathlon events, competitors have to cycle 180 kilometres. Triathlon bikes have handlebars with elbow pads to support the rider.

*Road racers should wear helmets, but some riders complain that they make them too hot.*

**Mountain-bike Racing**
Mountain bikes are very sturdy machines with rugged, knobbly tyres, strong brakes and lots of gears. These bikes are built to be ridden off the road, up steep slopes and through extremely rough terrain. An off-road race can get pretty tough, so bike and rider have to be in peak condition if they are going to finish.

*Cyclists wear skintight shorts and shirts. These keep the rider warm and streamlined.*

## The Great Race

The Tour de France is the greatest road race of all. Every year, hundreds of riders snake their way across France during this demanding 3,400-kilometre race. The top three riders are awarded a different-coloured jersey at the end of each day to show what part of the race they have done well in.

*Yellow jersey (leading rider)*

*Polka-dot jersey (most climbing points)*

*Green jersey (most sprint points)*

## Changing Gear

All bikes have the same basic shape, but wheel, frame, saddle and handlebar styles vary.

Mountain bike

Road-racing bike

Time-trial bike

Track-racing bike

## Life on the Road

Road race riders avoid stopping at all costs. They eat and drink on the move, and simple repairs are carried out by mechanics hanging out of cars that speed alongside the bikes.

*Riders apply special oils to their legs to keep the muscles and knee joints warm.*

*The riders shave their legs to make it easier to apply protective oils to their skin.*

*Racers wear special shoes that clip onto the bike's pedals. This helps the rider to pull the pedals up as well as push them down.*

# MOTOR SPORTS

When you watch a motor race your senses are bombarded by the event. The engines roar so loudly that you feel the ground shake. You smell burning rubber as tyres spin on tarmac. You watch mechanics desperately trying to keep their machines working. For both the drivers and the spectators there is no doubt that motor sport is one of the most exciting sporting experiences in the world.

### Rallying

Rally cars are based on road cars. Each car has a navigator and a driver. The navigator reads a map and, because the cars are so noisy, he uses a microphone to tell the driver which way to go.

*During a race, repairs are done in the pits. Mechanics work as fast as they can to get the car back into the race.*

*Drivers wear a helmet fitted with a microphone so that they can speak to the pit crew at all times.*

*A tyre change takes under eight seconds. The tyres are held on by special nuts that can be undone easily.*

*This car has wings at the front and back. At high speed, air rushes over the wings. The pressure of this air keeps the car on the ground.*

### Drag Racing

Drag-racing cars are designed to go as fast as possible in a straight line. They reach speeds of 470 kilometres an hour.

The car speeds down a track 400 metres long.

## Motorcycling

Racing motorcycles are extremely fast and have wide tyres and curved windscreens. The sport looks very dramatic because the bikes corner at such an amazing angle to the track that the rider's knees almost scrape the ground!

## Speedway

Speedway bikes race anticlockwise around an oval track with a loose, dry surface. The bikes corner at speeds of up to 110 kilometres an hour. But as they do not have brakes, the riders slide the bikes around the corners to slow down.

*These mechanics are wearing flameproof headgear because they are refuelling the car.*

*During a race the tyres get very hot. This makes them sticky and helps the car to grip the track.*

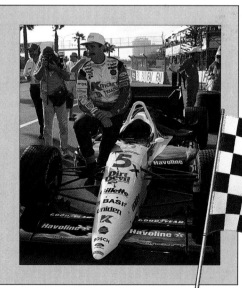

## Double Record

British driver Nigel Mansell is one of the greatest racing drivers of the 1980s and 1990s. In 1993 he became the only driver in history to be both Formula One and American IndyCar champion at the same time.

The only way of slowing the car down quickly once it crosses the finishing line . . .

. . . is by releasing a parachute!

*Finishing flag*

# SWIMMING

An Olympic-size swimming pool is 50 metres long, with eight lanes for the competitors to swim up and down in. Depending on whether they do front crawl, backstroke, breaststroke or butterfly, Olympic swimmers can compete over distances ranging from 50 to 1,500 metres. These swimmers train so hard that they spend most of their waking hours in a swimming pool.

**Super Swimmer**
In 1972 Mark Spitz made sporting history when he became the first competitor ever to win seven gold medals at one Olympics.

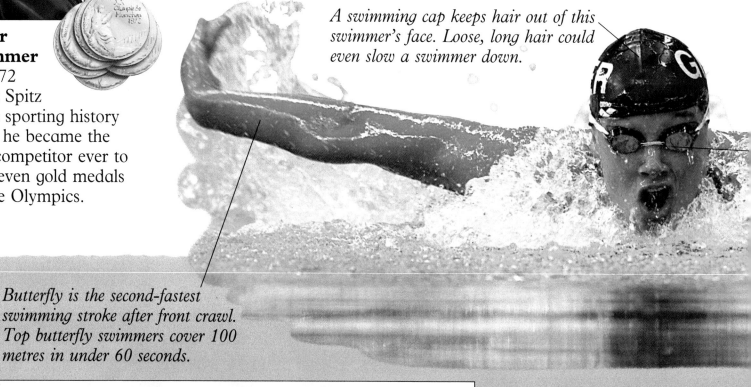

*A swimming cap keeps hair out of this swimmer's face. Loose, long hair could even slow a swimmer down.*

*Butterfly is the second-fastest swimming stroke after front crawl. Top butterfly swimmers cover 100 metres in under 60 seconds.*

**Water Polo**
Water polo is an exhausting game. Players need to be very confident swimmers as they have to control the ball with one hand. They are not allowed to punch the ball or to touch the bottom of the pool. Teams are identified by their white or blue caps. Goalkeepers wear red caps.

**Front crawl**

**Backstroke**

**Breaststroke**

**Butterfly**

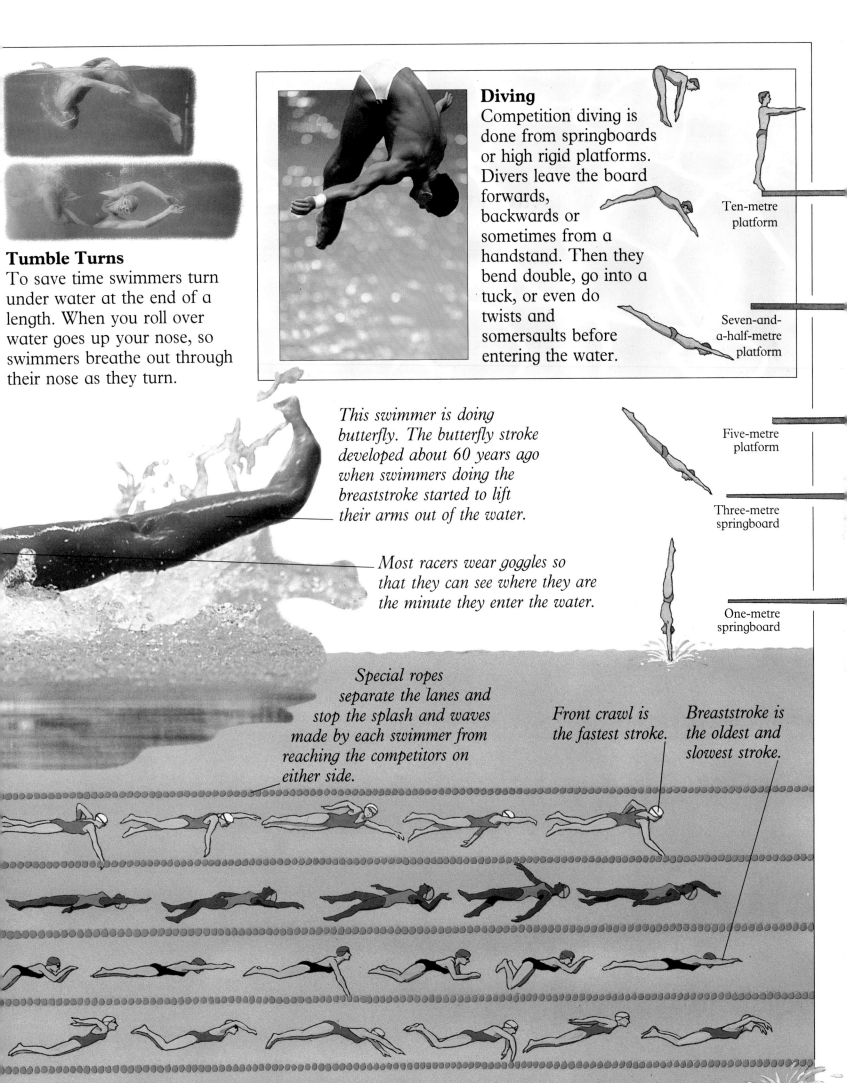

## Tumble Turns

To save time swimmers turn under water at the end of a length. When you roll over water goes up your nose, so swimmers breathe out through their nose as they turn.

## Diving

Competition diving is done from springboards or high rigid platforms. Divers leave the board forwards, backwards or sometimes from a handstand. Then they bend double, go into a tuck, or even do twists and somersaults before entering the water.

Ten-metre platform

Seven-and-a-half-metre platform

*This swimmer is doing butterfly. The butterfly stroke developed about 60 years ago when swimmers doing the breaststroke started to lift their arms out of the water.*

Five-metre platform

Three-metre springboard

*Most racers wear goggles so that they can see where they are the minute they enter the water.*

One-metre springboard

*Special ropes separate the lanes and stop the splash and waves made by each swimmer from reaching the competitors on either side.*

*Front crawl is the fastest stroke.*

*Breaststroke is the oldest and slowest stroke.*

43

# ROWING

On rivers, lakes and the sea you can employ one of the world's most incredible engines to power a craft across the water. That engine is – you! Using either paddles or oars you can get enormous satisfaction as your boat or canoe cuts through the water. You can also hoist sails to use the natural force of the wind to get a boat on the move.

## Sculling

Sculling is different to rowing because the competitors use two shorter oars (sculls) each rather than one longer oar.

*The blade is the part of the oar that pushes the water and moves the boat.*

*The oars are nearly four metres long. Long oars give greater pulling power, and help the boat to go faster.*

*The rower at the front moves the rudder at the other end of the boat by pulling wires with his feet.*

*Competition boats like this one are narrow and light so that they speed through the water.*

*Metal holders, called rowlocks, hold the oars out over the water.*

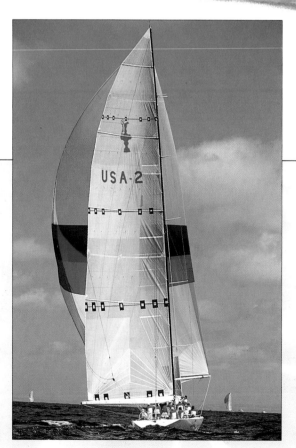

## Sailing

Sailing boats of many different sizes take part in competitions. They can sail across oceans or along inland waterways. But they all follow the same basic principle – positioning the sails so that they are filled by the wind. This moves the boat along.

*This gigantic America's Cup yacht needs a crew of over ten people.*

*This Laser 2 sailing dinghy can be sailed by one person. It is small enough to be transported on top of a car.*

## Canoeing

There are two different types of canoe – a kayak and a Canadian canoe. You sit in a kayak and use a paddle with a blade on each end. In a Canadian canoe you half-kneel and use a single-bladed paddle.

*Canadian canoe*

*Kayak*

*Slalom canoeists have to steer their way through a series of green gates. But if the gate is red, the canoeist has to go past it and paddle back up through it.*

*The oarsman at the back, called the stroke, sets the rhythm for the whole boat.*

*This indicator shows the direction of the rudder below. When the rudder is moved to the left or right the boat turns in the same direction.*

## The Boat Race

The rowing race between the English universities of Oxford and Cambridge first took place in 1829. The teams of eight rowers and a cox do battle every year over a 6.78-kilometre stretch of the River Thames.

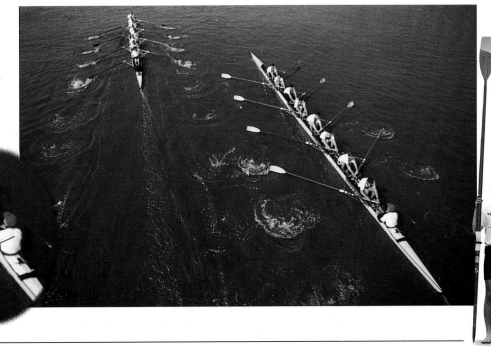

*The cox steers the boat and helps the team to row together.*

# WINDSURFING

The sea is one of the world's greatest natural sporting facilities. You can ride the waves on a board, with a sail or while being towed behind a boat. Windsurfing and surfing can be enjoyed during a holiday at the beach, but for some people these sports become a way of life as they search for ideal conditions or perfect waves.

*Plastic battens slide into pockets in the sail to help it keep its shape.*

*The boom goes around the mast and the sail. The windsurfer pulls on the boom to move the sail around and change direction.*

## One-design Racing
Competitors in the Olympic windsurfing course-racing event all have to use the same type of sail and board.

*Mast*

## Board Lengths
Beginners can use a funboard or a mid-length board. Slalom racers use a shorter board. Top slalom, wave and speed windsurfers often have a board specially made for them.

*Windsurfers often sail in cold weather, so they have to wear wetsuits to keep warm.*

Funboard

Mid-length board

Slalom board

Custom-made board

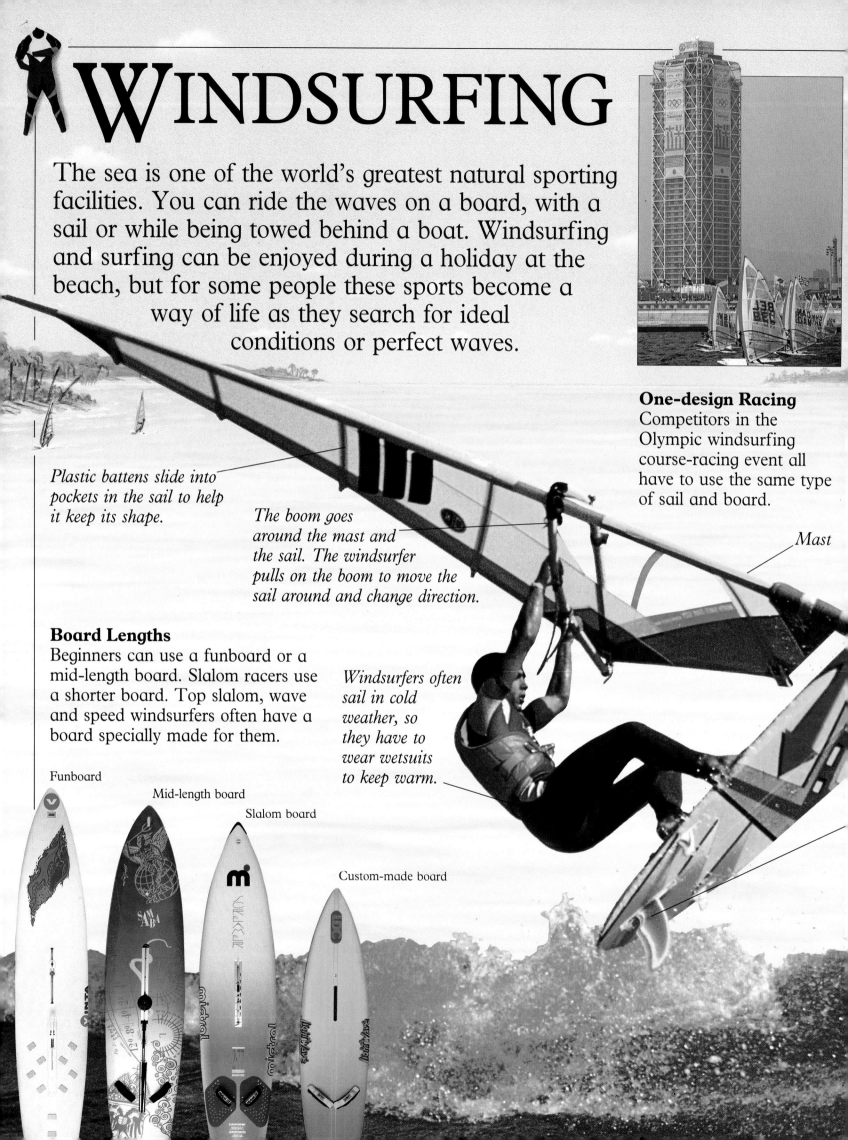

## Surfing

Surfers use a board to ride enormous waves as they roll towards the shoreline. An ultimate surfing move is to ride along the inside of the wave as the top curls right over you. This is known as riding the tube.

*Beginners can ride the waves lying on a body board.*

*This board is made to jump waves, so it is particularly short and light.*

## Riding the Wind

Windsurfers can take part in different competitions. They can race around a slalom course, do spectacular wave jumps or attempt speed records on really narrow boards, called speed needles.

*The fin, or skeg, helps to keep the board stable in the water.*

Slalom

Wave performance

Speed

## Water Skiing

Water skiers are towed behind a boat and use one or two skis. Slalom skiers use one ski and have to swing out behind the towing boat in order to ski around six marker buoys.

# WHO'S WHO?

Find out more about the athletes, players and teams featured in Picturepedia Sport.

## World of Sport
Cricket: *Salim Malik (Pakistan), Duchess of Norfolk XI vs Pakistan, Arundel, 1992;* Special Olympics: *Tanni Grey (GB), Barcelona 1992;* Winter Olympics: *Stephane Exartier (France), Albertville 1992;* Runner: *William Tanui (Kenya), IAAF/Mobil Grand Prix, Lausanne, 1992;* Showjumper: *Mark Todd (NZ) on Kleenex Face the Music, The Dubai Eventers Special 1991;* Diver: *Mingxia Fu (China), Barcelona 1992;* Tennis player: *Steffi Graf (Germany), Wimbledon 1993;* Athlete: *Carl Lewis (USA), Barcelona 1992.*

## Running
Relay: *Dennis Mitchell and Carl Lewis (USA), Barcelona 1992;* Steeplechase: *Kenyans Matthew Birir (1107), Patrick Sang (1138), William Mutwol (1133), Barcelona 1992;* 100 metres: *Merlene Ottey (Jamaica), World Championships, Tokyo, 1991;* Hurdles: *Colin Jackson (GB), European Championships, Split, 1990;* Start: *Giuseppina Cirulli (Italy), Los Angeles 1984;* Long distance: *Doina Melinte (Romania), IAAF/Mobil Grand Prix, Stockholm, 1992.*

## Decathlon
Pole vaulter: *Ian Tullett (GB) 1993;* Heptathlon: *Jackie Joyner-Kersee (USA), Seoul 1988.*

## Gymnastics
Rhythmic all-around: *Alexandra Timochenko (EUN), Barcelona 1992;* Beam: *Zsuzsanna Csisztu (Hungary), Seoul 1988;* Asymmetric bars: *Li Lu (China), World*

*Championships, Paris, 1992;* Rings: *Vitaliy Scherbo (EUN), World Championships, Birmingham, 1993.*

## Martial Arts
Judo: *Cecile Nowak (France) vs Ryoko Tamura (Japan), Barcelona 1992.*

## Archery
Archery: *Seoul 1988;* Shooting: *The Sultan of Brunei, Commonwealth Games, Auckland, 1990.*

## Golf
Golf: *Florence Descampe (Belgium), Dinah Shore Open, Mission Hills, 1993;* Snooker: *Stephen Hendry (GB), World Championships, Sheffield, 1992.*

## Tennis
Tennis: *Gretchen Magers (USA), Wimbledon 1989;* Pelota: *Biarritz (France) 1991;* Table tennis: *Li Huifen (China), English Open Championships, Brighton, 1988.*

## Basketball
Basketball: *Golden State Warriors vs Portland Trailblazers 1991;* Harlem Globetrotters: *Curly Johnson (USA) and fan;* Fashionable feet: *Michael Jordan (USA) playing for the Chicago Bulls;* Team handball: *Korea vs Norway, Barcelona 1992;* Volleyball: *Kent Steffes (USA) playing Pro Beach Volleyball.*

## Soccer
Soccer: *British players Gary McAllister in white (Leeds United) and Mark Hughes in red (Manchester United).*

## Rugby and American Football
American football: *Jim Everett (USA) quarterback for the LA Rams;* Rugby: *Christian Strauss (South*

*Africa), European Tour 1992;* The snap: *Mark Malone (USA) quarterback for the San Diego Chargers;* The scrum: *England vs Ireland;* Australian rules football: *Carlton vs North Melbourne.*

## Baseball
Baseball: *Boston Red Sox vs Milwaukee Brewers 1990;* Cricket: *England vs Pakistan, Lords 1992.*

## Ice Hockey
Ice hockey: *USA vs URS, Calgary 1988;* Goalkeeper: *France vs USA, Albertville 1992;* Roller hockey: *Holland vs Portugal, Barcelona 1992.*

## Figure Skating
Figure skating: *Sophie Moniotte and Pascal Lavanchy (France), European Championships, Lausanne, 1992;* Singles: *Chen Lu (China), Albertville 1992;* Pairs: *Cheryl Peake and Andrew Naylor (GB), Skate Electric International, Richmond, 1990;* Ice dance: *Stefania Calegari and Pasquale Camerlengo (Italy), World Championships, Prague, 1993;* Speed skating: *Emese Hunyady (Austria), Albertville 1992.*

## Skiing
Skiing: *Petra Kronberger (Austria), Lake Louise 1992;* Snowboard: *Avoriaz 1991;* Ski jump: *Calgary 1988;* Luge: *Susi Erdmann (Germany), World Championships 1993;* Bobsleigh: *Gustav Weder and Donat Acklin (Switzerland), Albertville 1992.*

## Three-Day Event
Three-day event: *Nicholas Holmes-Smith (Canada) on Espionage, Seoul 1988;* Dressage: *Mary Thomson (GB) on King William, Barcelona 1992;* Endurance: *Vicki Latta (NZ) on Chief, Barcelona 1992;* Polo: *West Palm Beach 1993.*

## Cycling
Tour de France: *Riding through Paris;* Life on the road: *Laudelino Cubino (Spain), Tour de France;* Mountain-bike racing: *Barrie Clarke (GB), Grundig MTB Championships, Belgium, 1992;* Track racing: *Chris Boardman (GB), Barcelona 1992.*

## Motor Sports
Racing car: *Danny Sullivan (USA), Indianapolis 500 1986;* Rallying: *Carlos Sainz (Spain) drives a Toyota, RAC Rally, GB, 1991;* Motorcycling: *Wayne Rainey (USA) on the Roberts Yamaha, British Grand Prix, Donington Park, 1992;* Speedway: *Erik Gundersen (Denmark) leads Jimmy Nilsen (Sweden).*

## Swimming
Swimming: *Franziska Van Almsick (Germany), European Championships, Sheffield, 1993;* Tumble turns: *Olympic gold medallist Sharron Davies, (GB);* Diver: *Greg Louganis (USA);* Water polo: *France vs Greece, Rome 1990.*

## Rowing
Rowing: *Coxless four, Salih Hassan, John Garrett, Gavin Stewart and Richard Stanhope (GB), Barcelona 1992.* Sculling: *Single sculls, Juri Jaanson (Estonia), Barcelona 1992;* Sailing: *Americas Cup 1991;* The boat race: *Hammersmith 1991.*

## Windsurfing
Windsurfing: *Hawaii;* One-design racing: *Barcelona 1992;* Slalom: *Slalom race, Hawaii 1990;* Wave performance: *Bjorn Dunkerbeck (Spain), World Championships, Fuerteventura, 1989;* Speed: *Eric Beale (GB), Les Saintes Maries de la Mer 1988;* Surfing: *Justin Strong (South Africa), Jeffrey Bay 1992.*

# INDEX

## Acknowledgments

**Photography:** Andy Crawford, The Colour Company, Kevin Mallet, Dave Rudkin.

**Additional photography:** Philip Gatward, Dave King, Tim Ridley, Chris Stevens.

**Illustrations:** Roy Flooks, Garden Studios, Linden Artists, Alex Pang.

**Thanks to:** John Jaques & Son Limited, Lillywhites, Norrie Carr Model Agency, Ocean Leisure, Olympus Sport, Leon Paul, Queens Ice Rink, Scallywags Model Agency, Jeremy Scoones, Tideway Scullers, Slick Willies, Soccer Scene.

## Picture credits

**Action Plus:** 16r, 21c, Chris Barry 33tr, Barrie Clarke 38bl, Mike Hewitt 30c, 42bl, Glyn Kirk 7c, 7bl, 19cr, 38tr, Eileen Langsley 12c, Peter Spurrier 44tl, P. Tarry 6bc, 6cr, George Tiederman 40/1c, Chris Van Lennep 47tc; **Allsport:** 21tc, 22br, 43tc, Bernard Asset 31tc, Chris Barry 33tc, C. Bernhardt 26c, Shaun Botteril 25tc & back jacket, Howard Boylan 8tl, 27c, 41tl, 41tr, 45br, Simon Bruty 6clb, 13cl, 42/3c & back jacket, David Cannon 19cl, Tony Duffy 9tl, 20bc, Stephen Dunn 18cr, Yann Guichaova 9tr, 12cl, 30tr, Mike Hewitt 23tr, Christian Le Bozec 46tr, Ken Levine 22cl, 23c, Caryn Levy 3c & 20/1c, Bob Martin 1c & 37br, 33br, Richard Martin 14/5c, 32/3c, 33tl, Gary Mortimore 7tr, 17tr, Stephen Munday 19tcr, 19tr, Adrian Murrell 29cr, Jon Nicholson 47c, Mike Powell 6c, 8cr, 30/1bc, 44bl, Ben Radford 24/5c, Pascal Rondeau 32cr & jacket, 35cr, Richard Saker 13tr, Ian Tomlinson 35c, 35tr; Anton Want 33tr; **Colorsport:** 6/7c, Biancotto 47cl, Valerie Desheulles 46/7c, Desheulles/Montiel 47cr, Bryan Yablonsky 28/9c; **Mary Evans:** 4cl & 10tl; **Guildford Spectrum:** 32tr; **Hulton:** 8cl, 8bl, 15crb, 16tl, 19tl, 19tcl, 20cla, 20c; **Image Bank:** Giuliano Colliva 24cl, Paolo Curto 42tr, Tom King 7tc; Grafton M. Smith endpapers; **Bob Langrish:** 36cr, 36/7c & jacket, 37tr; **Popperfoto:** 42tl; **Mark Shearman:** 10/11c; **Sporting Pictures:** Giuseppina Cirulli 4cla & 8br, 6tl, 7br, 9cl & jacket, 9cr, 11tl, 14cl, 20clb, 22/3tc, 27tr, 27bl, 27br, 31c, 34cl & jacket, 35tl, 38/9c, 39cl, 41c, 41br.

Every effort has been made to trace the copyright holders, and we apologize in advance for any unintentional omissions. We would be pleased to insert the appropriate acknowledgments in any subsequent edition of this publication.

| | | |
|---|---|---|
| t – **top** | l – **left** | a – **above** |
| b – **below** | r – **right** | c – **centre** |